passion
paths

Passion Paths

WILLIAM R. GRIMBOL
Worship Services for
Ash Wednesday and Holy Week

C.S.S. Publishing Co., Inc.
Lima, Ohio

PASSION PATHS

Copyright © 1987 by
The C.S.S. Publishing Company, Inc.
Lima, Ohio

You may copy the material in this publication if you are the original purchaser, for use as it was intended (worship material for worship use; educational material for classroom use; dramatic material for staging and production). No additional permission is required from the publisher for such copying by the original purchaser only. Inquiries should be addressed to: The C.S.S. Publishing Company, Inc., 628 South Main Street, Lima, Ohio 45804.

Library of Congress Cataloging-in Publications Data

Grimbol, William R., 1950-
    Passion paths.

    1. Lent. 2. Worship programs. 3. Holy Week services. 4. Easter service. I. Title.
BV85.G75 1987   264   86-25094
ISBN 0-89536-842-0

2/87 1T

7801 / ISBN 0-89536-842-0   PRINTED IN U.S.A.

Table of Contents

Author's Preface...................... 7

1. The Service for Ash Wednesday....... 9
   "The Path of Maturity"............. 13

2. The Service for Palm Sunday......... 19
   "The Path of Quality".............. 24

3. The Service for Maundy Sunday...... 31
   "The Path of Integrity"............ 39

4. The Service for Good Friday......... 43
   "The Path of Dignity".............. 46

5. The Service for Easter Day.......... 49
   "The Path of Creativity"........... 57

Author's Preface

This series of worship services and sermons, *Passion Paths,* strives to offer the congregation an exploration of certain concepts and words that seem to have eroded through misuse, or just a general lack of use. "Maturity" ... "Quality" ... "Integrity" ... "Dignity" ... "Creativity" are all words that we may choose to use, but we seldom have a deep understanding or firm comprehension of just exactly what we do mean by those terms. Lent is an ideal time for an examination of these concepts, for each takes on new life, vitality, energy and purpose when used or heard from the perspective of the Cross, or the context of the Resurrection. It is my hope that if these concepts can once again pack the symbolic and spiritual wallop that I believe is contained within them, than Lent, too, will take on a dynamic and dramatic tone and texture.

Lent is a time when we must dig down deep inside ourselves, in order to explore the scope of our sin, as well as the decay of our low level of discipleship. Such a rigorous venture will often leave us anxious and guilt-ridden and certain that we will never find our way out of this maze of mistakes. Each one of the passion paths illuminated in these services and sermons is a very real attempt to help us make what Edna Hong chose to call, in her book of the same title, a "downward ascent." These passion paths offer the congregation a means of entering the deepest needs and hurts and flaws and failings of the Self, but also to rise up again with new courage and commitment, and to exit the labors of Lent on the wings of an "eastering" ascent.

The responsive readings in these services can definitely use a lay leader rather than the pastor, and one should feel free to use lay participants for any part of the service where it is believed to be appropriate. The services are certainly written with the intention of being as flexible as possible in this regard.

The dramatic readings should be done without costuming, any significant staging, or any other typical theater trappings. The goal is to be stark and simple, and to retain the sermonic look and feel. I should suggest simply the use of a spotlight, or some other very basic device to call attention to the various readers.

8

THE SERVICE
FOR ASH WEDNESDAY

PRELUDE

CALL TO WORSHIP
Pastor: We come this [day/night] to get in tune and in touch, with our hearts — our spirits — our souls.
People: **Free us, O God, to go down deep inside ourselves, and to penetrate the core of love at our center.**
Pastor: Enable us, O God, to make the downward ascent during this mysterious and miraculous Lenten season.
People: **Lent is a painful time of fearless examination, and yet, also a time of significant renewal.**
All: *We come ready for both the scrutiny and the restoration, ready to go down inside ourselves, as well as up into the eternal embrace of your love. Amen*

HYMN: *"Beneath the Cross of Jesus"*

SILENT CONFESSION

THE WORDS OF ABSOLUTION
Pastor: Whenever we feel that our lives are as barren and brittle as a naked tree in the midst of winter, remind us, Lord, that beneath the surface of our souls, your molten grace is preparing the blossoms and buds of a forever spring. Remind us, Lord, that your forgiveness heals and renews us, even when we cannot sense your presence.
People: **We give thanks for the gift of your love,
a gift which comforts and consoles,
a gift which cauterizes and confronts,
a gift which resurrects our energy and excitement
   for life. Amen**

SCRIPTURE READING: *Psalm 90*

ANTHEM / SOLO

SCRIPTURE READING: *Ephesians 4:1-16*

HYMN: *"In the Cross of Christ I Glory"*

THE SERMON: *"The Path of Maturity"* . . . *A Dramatic Reading*

QUIET MEDITATION

OFFERING

OFFERTORY

LITANY
Pastor: We have myriad excuses for our failure to love, O Christ, and even we are weary of them.
People: Grant us the courage and the conviction
to never stop working on our loving . . .
to never stop listening . . .
to never stop caring . . .
to never stop forgiving . . .
to never stop embracing . . .
to never stop granting to others our understanding — our respect — our compassion . . .
to never stop believing in the power of love
to bind the brokenhearted,
to heal and make whole,
to create an abundant hope.
All: *To love is our greatest calling.*
To love is our greatest challenge.
To love is our greatest triumph.
To love is our greatest testimony of faith. Amen

THE SACRAMENT OF THE LORD'S SUPPER

WORDS OF PREPARATION
Pastor: As we celebrate communion this day/night, let us be scorched with the awareness that to lead a life of mature loving will, as it did for Christ, require all that we are. Let us be scalded with the consciousness that mature loving always leads to a cross.

THE WORDS OF INSTITUTION
"Come to me, all who labor and are heavy laden, and I will give you rest." *(Matthew 11:28 RSV)*

That invitation still stands for the followers of Jesus. He is here, he is the host for this meal. He is the one who promises us forgiveness. He is the one who assures us of eternal life. We are his disciples, and as we gather around this table, our faith in him binds us together as brothers and sisters.

Hear the words from the upper room:

"In the night in which he was betrayed, our Lord Jesus took bread, and gave thanks; broke it, and gave it to his disciples, saying, 'Take and eat; this is my body, given for you. Do this for the remembrance of me'."

THE COMMUNION

THE LORD'S PRAYER

THE PASSING OF THE PEACE

UNISON READING: *1 Corinthians 12:31; chapter 13; 14:1a*

Earnestly desire the higher gifts.
And I will show you a still more excellent way.
If I speak in the tongues of men and of angels, but have not love, I am a noisy gong or a clanging cymbal. And if I have prophetic powers, and understand all mysteries and all knowledge, and if I have all faith, so as to remove mountains, but have not love, I am nothing. If I give away all I have, and if I deliver my body to be burned, but have not love, I gain nothing.

Love is patient and kind; love is not jealous or boastful; it is not arrogant or rude. Love does not insist on its own way; it is not irritable or resentful; it does not rejoice at wrong, but rejoices in the right. Love bears all things, believes all things, hopes all things, endures all things.

Love never ends, as for prophecy, it will pass away; as for tongues, they will cease; as for knowledge, it will pass away. For our knowledge is imperfect and our prophecy is imperfect; but when the perfect comes, the imperfect will pass away. When I was a child, I spoke like a child, I thought like a child, I reasoned like a child; when I became a man, I gave up childish ways. For now we see in a mirror dimly, but then face to face. Now I know in part; then I shall understand fully, even as I have been fully understood. So faith, hope, love abide, these three; but the greatest of these is love.

HYMN: *"When I Survey the Wondrous Cross"*

BENEDICTION

Pastor: Let us depart in peace, emboldened by the cross to be reckless and rigorous in our loving. And let our loving always reflect the maturity which that cross demands of all disciples. Amen

POSTLUDE

The Path of Maturity

READER 1

Somehow, Lord, everywhere we look in Scripture,
the concept of maturity is always fused with our capacity to
   love,
and our capacity to love is always bonded to our ability
to first love ourselves.
Why? Why did you have to make the task of maturation
so brutally simple . . . so crucifyingly modest?
Why does our maturation migration always have to wing its
   way home
to the context of loving . . . the art of loving . . . the work
   of loving?
It is just such a naive notion . . .
   such an idealistic and sentimental vision . . .
   such an exercise in hopeless frustration.
If our maturity is always to be measured by the
extent and depth of our commitment to loving, well, then
we are all hopelessly destined to lives of foolishness and
   childishness.
Even at the beginning we are utter failures . . .
to love our Selves . . . impossible!

Lord, we have so much to dislike in our Selves,
so much we find pathetic and phony and false.
We are possessed by possessions.
We are addicted to accumulation.
We hide behind ridiculous images — masks — titles — brands.
We have grown callous to what we feel.
We have grown bored with what we think.
We have grown indifferent to what we believe.
We seldom ever dream . . . set new goals . . . make new friends,
or even seem able to embrace and enjoy life.

For most of us, life is just an endurance test
which nobody passes, and the most we can hope for
is to endure . . . to kill some time . . . waste some time
. . . spend some time.
Who could have ever imagined that Time would become our
   most feared enemy?

We are ashamed, Lord, of our laziness . . . our lack of courage
   . . . our lack of hope . . . our lack of faith.
We are embarrassed with how little time we actually
devote to the art of loving . . . how seldom we strive to fulfill
your call to love with reckless abandon, but Lord,
we just don't love our Selves, we just don't believe
that our lives are really worth that much . . . we just don't
   believe
that life has all that much to offer, except the good life,
and that is so bankrupt ethically, because it has nothing
   whatsoever
to do with goodness. We must start with our Selves,
but there just seems to be so little there worth loving . . .
so little there for which we feel genuine pride . . .
so little there for which we feel You might be proud.
Maturity? Loving? We fall so miserably short.

READER 2

Next, You ask us to love our neighbor as our Self.
Our neighbor . . . who is that?
There once was a time when we sat on front porches,
and chatted with our neighbors, but these days
we hide behind backyard fences, and screened-in patios.
We fear our neighbors.
They are our competition. They are our opponents
in the mad scramble up the ladder of success.
Our neighbors might find out our flaws or our failings,
they might uncover our fragility and vulnerability,

or they might expose the frightening child that lurks within
that tough and together exterior.
Our neighbors are not to be trusted.
They might steal our piece of the pie.
They might get a higher rank on the success ladder.
They might wear more designer labels.
Loving our neighbors, well, Lord, once again
You prove how out of touch and unaware You
are of reality . . . the real world.

READER 3

When it comes to loving the world, You just
expect too much . . . way, way too much.
You were such an idealist; I mean, You loved
anybody and everybody, regardless of status or position . . .
      regardless of role or rank . . .
      regardless of color or religion . . .
      regardless of sin or crime.
As sensible religious folks, we claim to love these outcasts,
but we are smart enough to not go near them,
so we don't get smudged or stained by their "loser" qualities,
or by their flagrant flaws, or their massive mistakes.
You, why You went right into their midst,
right into the middle of that moral squalor, and You
kept on celebrating the miracles You insisted that You found
in all of that bland boring mundane existence.
Such an idealist!

READER 4

You even had the gall to ask us, to ask us to love our enemies.
What mature person really loves their enemies?
Not any mature person I know.
Were You a pacifist? Honest, I mean if You
really meant it, to love our enemies, then You
had to be . . . bottom line . . . a pacifist.

Loving our enemies means giving up our weapons . . .
> our weaponry of grudges and resentments . . .
> our weaponry of past injustices and humiliations . . .
> our weaponry of known defects and inadequacies in others . . .
> our weaponry of righteous indignation and smug morality . . .
> our weaponry of superior intellect and aristocratic arrogance . . .
> our weaponry of warmaking . . . the bombs and bullets that now threaten to blast Creation back to chaos again.

Do You really expect us to give up our weapons?
Do You really expect us to be peacemakers?
Do You really expect us to love our enemies . . .
which means knowing them . . . understanding them . . . accepting them . . .
living side by side with them . . . respecting them . . . forgiving them . . .
LOVING THEM?

READER 5

Christ did mean it . . . He meant exactly what he said,
and that call to radical — reckless — rigorous loving
remains to this day the most troublesome message of his ministry.
Christ has called us all to pass the acid test of faith,
which is to always keep on widening the scope of our loving,
and to know that our loving is also that which
serves as a sacred symbol of our maturity,
as a sign of our growing up into Christ,
who is the Author of all loving.

Christ did mean it, but he also meant that
if we will only work on our loving relationship with Him,
the love will burst forth out of us like lava from a volcano.

If we will only work, and I mean work,
at our intimacy with Christ . . . our prayer life . . .
    our study of Scripture . . .
    our peacemaking . . .
    our pursuit of justice . . .
    our service and our sacrifice . . .
    our forgiving and being forgiven . . .
    our tender mercies, administered to a tortured and troubled world.

then, and only then, can we fulfill the mature call to obedient loving;
then, and only then, can we find within ourselves the courage necessary
to pick up our crosses and follow . . . follow Him who is our Lord and Savior.

He meant it!

He meant every word!

    There is simply no denying the truth that maturity and loving are like spiritual Siamese twins, and that discipleship is the life lived by those who know the spiritual seal of those fused and bonded concepts and actions.
    Maturity and loving, they are one and the same, and one without the other is like a Cross without a Resurrection, or an Easter without a Good Friday.

18

THE SERVICE FOR PALM SUNDAY

PRELUDE

CALL TO WORSHIP
Pastor: We come to worship this day, so profoundly grateful.
People: **Grateful that you arrived in Jerusalem that day as the prince of peace, and not as a champion of war. Grateful that you arrived in Jerusalem that day in a posture of humility, and not a position of pompous pride. Grateful that you so passionately believed in the truth, that the demonic eyes of the cross could not stare you down.**
All: *What penetrating and powerful thanksgiving we bring to this service of worship, what adoration we feel within. Amen*

RESPONSIVE READING: *Psalm 95:1-7a; 96*
O come, let us sing to the Lord;
> **Let us make a joyful noise to the rock of our salvation!**

Let us come into his presence with thanksgiving;
> **Let us make a joyful noise to him with songs of praise!**

For the Lord is a great God,
> **And a great King above all gods,**

In his hand are the depths of the earth; the heights of the mountains are his also.
> **The sea is his, for he made it; for his hands formed the dry land.**

O come, let us worship and bow down, let us kneel before the Lord, our Maker!
> **For he is our God, and we are the people of his pasture, and the sheep of his hand.**

O sing to the Lord a new song;
> **Sing to the Lord, all the earth!**

Declare his glory among the nations,
> **His marvelous works among all the peoples!**

For great is the Lord, and greatly to be praised;
> **He is to be feared above all gods.**

For all the gods of the peoples are idols;
> **But the Lord made the heavens.**

Honor and majesty are before him;
> **Strength and beauty are in his sanctuary.**

Ascribe to the Lord, O families of the peoples,
> **Ascribe to the Lord glory and strength!**

Ascribe to the Lord the glory due his name;
> **Bring an offering, and come into his courts!**

Worship the Lord in holy array;
> **Tremble before him, all the earth!**

Say among the nations, "The Lord reigns!
> **Yes, the world is established, it shall never be moved; he will judge the peoples with equity."**

Let the heavens be glad, and let the earth rejoice;
> **Let the sea roar, and all that fills it;**

Let the field exult, and everything in it!
> **Then shall all the trees of the wood sing for joy before the Lord,**

For he comes, for he comes to judge the earth.
> **He will judge the world with righteousness, and the peoples with his truth.**

HYMN: *"All Glory, Laud, and Honor"*
(A Procession of Palms)

THE PRAYER OF CONFESSION

Pastor: O God, forgive us for our woeful lack of passion.
People: We fail so often to feel our convictions deeply . . .
to express our faith concretely . . .
to witness to your grace with acts of mercy . . .
to enter into the world with courage . . .
to embrace the world with compassion . . .
to enable peace and justice to reign on earth as it must in heaven

Pastor: O God, forgive us for our woeful lack of passion.
People: We have strayed from the path of passion, and

	wound up hopelessly lonely and lost on roads that lead only to apathy and indifference . . .
	to hopelessness and despair . . .
	to decay and decadence . . .
	to spiritual deadness.
All:	*We desperately need an infusion of passion, Lord, so that we might regain our sense of urgency . . .*
	our sense of purpose . . .
	our strength of faith . . .
	our power and our peace.
	All of which can come only from you, dear Christ.
	Amen

THE WORDS OF ASSURANCE

A SPECIAL READING: *"Com-Passion"*

Compassion is to me simply defined as the willingness and desire to spiritually sneak inside the "flesh-coat" of another human being, and then allow oneself to consciously feel the texture of the cloak of their humanity. The compassionate person carefully surveys this spiritual weave, diligently trying to ascertain where are the tension sags, the sources of tautness, the wrinkles of worry, the patches that cover pain, and even the worn spots that need the mending of affirmation. The compassionate person is not afraid to pour himself or herself into a temporal tunic that is as tight as a vice from long-term hurt or abuse, emotional or physical, nor is he or she wary of wearing, for a time, the tattered skins of those whom society has branded as outcasts.

That which most often prevents us from experiencing compassion is fear . . . fear of genuinely and fully sympathizing with another human being. We fear the lonely face in the nursing home, that quietly sighs in the agony of only having memories to live on. We fear the black face that represents a culture and heritage we find foreign and which we judge as primitive and barbaric. We fear the Jewish face that tells of a faith that is deep and sure and strong, and often leaves us doubting the depth of our own commitment. We fear the adolescent face that radiates joy one minute, rage the next, cynical doubt the next, and the need to forget what Life feels like much of the time. We fear the face of depression, the face that shows no hint of hope, no possibility of dreams. We fear the anxious face, the face that reveals a waiting volcanic eruption of anger or tears, a face that strikes too often too close to home.

As Christians we must overcome our fear through faith in Christ. We must come to realize that we will find peace internally for ourselves, only when there is peace inside for our neighbor as well. Compassion is the catalyst for love, it is the motor which keeps the work of loving going, and it is the well from which Christ draws the power of faith. Compassion waters the human soul with care and kindness, fertilizes it by taking its needs and wants seriously, and enables the flower that is within to bloom.

William R. Grimbol

ANTHEM / SOLO

SCRIPTURE LESSON: *Luke 19:28-40*

HYMN: *"Crown Him With Many Crowns"* or *"Ride On, Ride On In Majesty"*

SERMON: *"The Path of Quality"* . . . *A Dramatic Reading*

THE OFFERING

THE OFFERTORY

THE LITANY

Pastor: Fill us with an abundant passion, O God,
People: **So that we might be inspired to feed the hungry, clothe the naked, and bind the brokenhearted.**
Pastor: Coat us in a layer of your love, O God,
People: **So that we might fulfill mightily your call to bring justice and peace to this good earth.**
Pastor: Arm us only with the weapon of wisdom, O God,
People: **So that we might still see the truth, even in the midst of ethical laziness and moral squalor.**
Pastor: Feed us with a large helping of your grace, O God,
People: **So that we might at last know satisfaction, serenity, the peace that does pass all understanding.**
Pastor: Renew us with the model of your passionate courage, O God,
People: **So that we might face our own Jerusalems, our own crosses, with a firm and steadfast faith.**
All: *Amen*

THE LORD'S PRAYER

HYMN: *"Lead On, O King Eternal"*

BENEDICTION

POSTLUDE

The Path of Quality

READER 1

We have, all of us, at some point, asked,
"Why did He go into Jerusalem on the back of an ass,
knowing full well that the symbolism of the event
would only serve as a catalyst for his own crucifixion?"
We have all wondered whether or not
Christ could not have played it smarter,
and avoided this whole atoning mess of the Cross.
I mean really, could not God have offered us a Son
who would have lived to a nice old age . . .
    died a nice peaceful death . . .
    in his sleep . . .
    at ninety years of age?
Why not? He still could have died for our sins,
but why did He have to have such a brutal finish . . .
    such a harsh ending?
Haven't we all wondered, deep down inside our Selves,
if the "pricetag" for atonement was too steep . . .
    too unfair
    unfair to Christ, and to us all?

READER 2

We have indeed spiritually struggled,
just like the people of His own time,
as to why we have to have a crucified Messiah.
We can handle the death of a Messiah,
but the crucifixion seems so extreme . . .
    so radical
    so unnecessary.
My own answer to this haunting question,
or my own effort to pass this eternal faith test,

has really evolved out of my own experience and observation of Life.
For me . . . well . . . I believe that Christ entered Jerusalem, at the peak Passover tourist season, on the back of an ass, because there was, quite simply, NO WAY TO AVOID THE CROSS.
Too stark . . . too simple . . . too sentimental an answer?
Sorry, but if, as I believe, that Christ's entire Life is a testimony to the Truth, then the Truth revealed here is this . . . Life is at times brutal and unfair, and that the true test of those who choose to follow that Truth, is whether or not they can in fact embrace the "givenness" of Life . . . the God authored reality . . . the human condition.

That is my answer, not a solution,
but a statement of faith . . .
my understanding of the Truth of Life . . . of Christ . . . of the Cross.
Maybe some of these others can explain it better . . .
 or more fully . . .
 or more, well, let them try.

READER 3

Let me try.
At no point in all of Scripture does Christ
ever seek to escape his humanness,
does he ever run from the confrontation or the conflict,
does he fail to accept Life on Life's terms.
Sure, Christ has his moment of doubt . . .
even a dab of despair here and there,
but the true miracle of his being,
the true nature of his divinity,
is that he ceaselessly and relentlessly chose
to embrace the givenness of Life . . .
 reality . . .
 the very raw human condition.

The Cross, for Christ, was just another sample of that
   commitment,
of that insistence on facing up to Life honestly — humanly
   — humbly,
but with divinely inspired courage.

The Cross, rather than being the dramatic pinnacle event
of obedience, is to me the fitting finale
of an entire life of such obedience,
the quiet epilogue to a play — a script — that is a testimony
   to the Truth,
the Truth that it is the will of God for
HUMANS TO BE HUMAN . . . it is the will of God
for humanity to embrace the fullness and the wholeness of Life
   . . .
it is the will of God for Paradise to contain a serpent,
and for Christ's life to contain *the* Cross,
and for our lives to contain myriad crosses.

READER 4

Maybe for all of us this Palm Sunday,
there is a need to assess and address our own passionate desire
to *remove* the passion from our lives . . .
to *avoid* the conflicts . . . to *deny* the risks . . .
to *eliminate* the needed confrontations . . .
to *skip over* the mistakes that beg for correction,
or the sins that beg for forgiving.
Maybe we all need to finally face
how frequently we want Life on our terms,
   in our control,
and void of any signs of the human condition.

Maybe we all need to experience the Lenten perspective
which frees us to at last know how much of our lives
are spent avoiding Life . . . escaping Life . . . candy-coating
   Life,

or merely choosing to be "dead" inside to the realities
of our times — our world — our lives.
Maybe we can prepare ourselves for the new life of Easter,
by facing the stale stagnant old life
of avoiding or eliminating those very life emotions and
experiences
that might force us to grow . . .
   to mature . . .
   to deepen . . .
   to sensitize . . .
   to celebrate . . .
   to rejoice . . .
   to worship . . .
   to adore . . .
   to dream . . .

to find in Life a quality . . . a quality that sparks our
energy and enthusiasm for Life . . . a quality
that in fact gives Life quality.
Maybe it is time for us all to admit that the boredom . . .
   the loneliness . . .
   the anxiety . . .
   the phoniness . . .
   the futility . . .
   the lack of quality living
we so often feel inside,
is due in large part to our own unwillingness to pick up our
   crosses,
   our own incessant choice of shallow living . . .
   cheap Grace . . . discipleship without discipline . . .
   the Good Life without goodness.
Maybe the greatest testimony to the Truth
is indeed the Cross, for without its symbolic scorching demand
to face Life head-on, we would all still be spending
most of our lives hiding,
hiding from the very thing that gives quality to our living,

hiding from the very thing that Christ chose
to defiantly . . . daily . . . diligently celebrate . . .
his humanness . . . his life . . . Life itself.

READER 5

On Palm Sunday
we reach inside ourselves . . . inside our faith . . .
and celebrate the courage of Christ,
his courage to enter Jerusalem knowing full well
that the end was well within sight.
Rather than avoiding the Truth,
which was the reality of the Cross,
Christ embraces the full potential and possibility of the event,
he embraces the Cross in faith.
Christ knew that a life that avoids the path of passion,
the way of the heart, the way of faith . . .
a life that rejects the service —
    the suffering —
    the sacrifices —
which enables that passion and any accompanying
    compassion . . .
is no life at all . . .
it is a dead life . . .
a hollow life . . .
a stagnant life . . .
a shallow life . . .
a childish life . . .
a life that has no QUALITY whatsoever.
On Palm Sunday we celebrate the path of passion,
    the path of quality,
    and we stand naked
    before the power
    of that passionate revealer of
    all that gives life
    QUALITY.

READER 6

Almost every day,
we too stand on the threshold of our own Jerusalems . . .
   before our own crosses . . .
   and we too have to make that choice
   of entering or avoiding.
We too, whether we be conscious of it or not,
are daily met with the faith-laden opportunity
to accept the givenness of Life . . .
to face the conflict . . .
to address the issue . . .
to respond to the crisis . . .
to cope with the suffering . . .
to celebrate the courage and the conviction.
Think about it . . . think of the friendships that await
the risk of healing words of forgiveness . . .
think of the marriages that wait for
silences to be at last addressed,
the lines of communication finally opened . . .
think of the families that anxiously wait for someone
to admit the anger — the hurt — the pain — even the love
   — the joy . . .
think of the lives that sit "dead" and dreary
wondering if they will ever face
the alcoholism — the incest — the compulsive gambling or
   eating —
the abuse of children or mates . . .
think of the grief never faced . . .
the priorities never sorted . . .
the dreams never actualized . . .
think of the mouths still waiting to be fed . . .
the peace still searching for makers . . .
think of the passionate denial of our possession by possessions,
   our addiction to accumulation . . .
think, just think,

of how many times a day Life invites us
to be enmeshed fully in her reality,
to embrace the givenness of her terms,
and to celebrate the tingling and triumphant courage
of those who choose the path of quality . . .
    those who choose to be fully and vibrantly alive.

READER 7

It is Palm Sunday,
and we rejoice and give thanks
for the triumphant testimony of the path of quality, a
    passion path
which leads to a Cross,
a path which opens to us all the way of wholeness,
the capacity to not just cope but to celebrate,
and the ability to say to Life, not
"Is that all there is?" but rather,
"My God, there is just so much . . . so much to live . . .
    to love . . .
    to learn.

Let us enter Jerusalem with Him,
and find in that Holy City,
the quality of Life we all so deeply yearn for . . .
    we all so passionately long to find.
        Amen

THE SERVICE
FOR MAUNDY THURSDAY

PRELUDE

CALL TO WORSHIP

Pastor: We gather here this night with humble and contrite hearts.
People: **We come as people who understand in faith, the integrity of washing feet.**
Pastor: We are aware, O God, of the beauty and the dramatic defiance of this symbol.
People: **We are aware, O God of your call to be servants to all people everywhere.**
All: *We come ready to heed your call, and ready to worship the integrity of your mission and your ministry, of your will and your word for our lives. Amen*

HYMN: *"There Is a Balm in Gilead"*

LITANY OF CONFESSION *(From* The Worshipbook, *Westmister Press, 1970 Joint Committee on Worship for Presbyterian Churches, pp. 109-110)*

Leader: Almighty God, you alone are good and holy. Purify our lives and make us brave disciples. We do not ask you to keep us safe, but to keep us loyal, so we may serve Jesus Christ, who, tempted in every way as we are, was faithful to you.
People: Amen.
Leader: From lack of reverence for truth and beauty; from a calculating or sentimental mind; from going along with mean and ugly things;
People: O God, deliver us.
Leader: From cowardice that dares not face truth; laziness content with half-truth; or arrogance that thinks it knows it all;
People: O God, deliver us.
Leader: From artificial life and worship; for all that is hollow or insincere;
People: O God, deliver us.

Leader: From trite ideals and cheap pleasures; from mistaking hard vulgarity for humor;
People: **O God, deliver us.**
Leader: From being dull, pompous, or rude; from putting down neighbors;
People: **O God, deliver us.**
Leader: From cynicism about our brothers; from intolerance or cruel indifference;
People: **O God, deliver us.**
Leader: From being satisfied with things as they are, in the church or in the world; from failing to share your indignation;
People: **O God, deliver us.**
Leader: From selfishness, self-indulgence, or self-pity;
People: **O God, deliver us.**
Leader: From token concern for the poor, for lonely or loveless people; from confusing faith with good feeling, or love with a wanting to be loved;
People: **O God, deliver us.**
Leader: For everything in us that may hide your light;
People: **O God, light of life, forgive us.**

DECLARATION OF PARDON

OLD TESTAMENT LESSON: *Psalm 23*

ANTHEM / SOLO

NEW TESTAMENT LESSON: *1 Corinthians 5:6-8*

SERMON: *"The Path of Integrity"* . . . *A Dramatic Reading*

HYMN: *"Amazing Grace! How Sweet the Sound"*

NICENE CREED

THE OFFERING

THE OFFERTORY

LITANY OF THE BEATITUDES: *(From* The Worshipbook, *Westminster Press, 1970 Joint Committee on Worship for Presbyterian Churches, pp. 105-108)*

Leader: Jesus said: Happy are the poor in spirit; theirs is the kingdom of heaven.

God our Father: help us to know that away from you we have nothing. Save us from pride that mistakes your gifts for possessions; and keep us humble enough to see that we are poor sinners who always need you.

People: **Happy are the poor in spirit.**

Leader: Thank you, God, for your Son Jesus, who, though he was rich, became poor to live among us; who had no place for himself on earth. By his weakness we are made strong, and by his poverty, rich.

Happy are the poor in spirit;

People: **Theirs is the kingdom of heaven.**

Leader: Jesus said: Happy are those who mourn; they shall be comforted.

God our Father: we are discouraged by evil and frightened by dying, and have no word of hope within ourselves. Unless you speak to us, O God, we shall be overcome by grieving and despair.

People: **Happy are those who mourn.**

Leader: Thank you, God, for Jesus Christ, who on the cross faced evil, death, and desertion. You raised him in triumph over every dark power to be our Savior. We give thanks for the hope we have in him.

Happy are those who mourn;

People: **They shall be comforted.**

Leader: Jesus said: Happy are the gentle; they shall have the earth.

God our Father: restrain our arrogance and show us

our place on earth. Keep us obedient, for we are your servants, unwise and unworthy, who have no rights and deserve no honors.

Happy are the gentle.
People: **They shall have the earth.**
Leader: Jesus said: Happy are those who hunger and thirst for what is right; they shall be satisfied.

God our Father: stir up in us a desire for justice, and a love of your law. May we never live carelessly or selfishly, but in all our dealing with neighbors may we look for the right and do it.
People: **Happy are those who hunger and thirst for what is right.**
Leader: Thank you, God, for Jesus Christ, who overturned small man-made rules, yet lived your law in perfect love. Give us freedom to live with your Spirit in justice, mercy, and peace.

Happy are those who hunger and thirst for what is right;
People: **They shall be satisfied.**
Leader: Jesus said: Happy are the merciful; they shall have mercy shown them.

God our Father: we do not forgive as you have forgiven us. We nurse old wrongs and let resentments rule us. We tolerate evil in ourselves, yet harshly judge our neighbors. God, forgive us.
People: **Happy are the merciful.**
Leader: Thank you, God, for your Son Jesus, who gave his life for sinners; who on the cross forgave unforgivable things. Receiving his mercy, may we always forgive.

Happy are the merciful.
People: **They shall have mercy shown them.**
Leader: Jesus said: Happy are the pure in heart; they shall see God.

God our Father: we are not pure. We do not live in love. The good we do, we admire too much; we tabulate our virtues. Deliver us, O God, from a divided heart.

People: **Happy are the pure in heart.**
Leader: Thank you, God, for Jesus Christ, whose words and deeds were pure. By his life our lives are justified, and by his death we are redeemed. In him we see you face to face, and praise you for your goodness.

Happy are the pure in heart;
People: **They shall see God.**
Leader: Jesus said: Happy are the peacemakers; they shall be called sons of God.

God our Father: we have not lived in peace. We have spread discord, prejudice, gossip, and fear among neighbors. Help us, for we cannot help ourselves. Show us your ways of peace.

People: **Happy are the peacemakers.**
Leader: Thank you, God, for Jesus Christ, who has broken down dividing walls of hate to make one family on earth. As he has reconciled us to you, may we be reconciled to one another, living in peace with all your children everywhere.

Happy are the peacemakers;
People: **They shall be called sons of God.**
Leader: Jesus said: happy are those who are persecuted in the cause of right; theirs is the kingdom of heaven.

God our Father: we are afraid to risk ourselves for the right. We have grown accustomed to wrong and been silent in the face of injustice. Give us anger without hate, and courage to obey you no matter what may happen.

People: **Happy are those who are persecuted in the cause of right.**

Leader: Thank you, God, for Jesus Christ, who was persecuted for what he said and did; who took the cross upon himself for our sake. May we stand with him in justice and love, and follow where he leads, even to a cross.

Happy are those who are persecuted in the cause of right.

People: **Theirs is the kingdom of heaven.**
Leader: Jesus said: Happy are you when people abuse you and persecute you and speak all kinds of evil against you on my account. Rejoice and be glad, for your reward will be great in heaven.

God our Father: give us a will to live by your commandments. Keep us from slander, cruelty, and mocking talk, so that we may be faithful witnesses to Jesus Christ our Lord.

People: **Happy are you when people abuse you and persecute you and speak all kinds of evil against you on my account.**
Leader: We praise you, O God, for your Son Jesus, who called us to be disciples. Give us grace to confess him before men, and faith to believe he suffered for us. We ask no rewards, only make us brave.

Happy are you when people abuse you and persecute you and speak all kinds of evil against you on my account.

People: **Rejoice and be glad, for your reward will be great in heaven.**
Leader: You are the light of the world. Your light must shine in the sight of men, so that, seeing your good works, they may give praise to your Father in heaven.
People: **Amen**

INVITATION TO THE LORD'S TABLE

"Come to me, all who labor and are heavy laden, and I will give you rest." (Matthew 11:28 RSV)

That invitation still stands for the followers of Jesus. He is here, he is the host for this meal. He is the one who promises us forgiveness. He is the one who assures us of eternal life. We are his disciples, and as we gather around this table, our faith in him binds us together as brothers and sisters.

Hear the words from the uppper room:

"In the night in which he was betrayed, our Lord Jesus took bread, and gave thanks; broke it, and gave it to his disciples, saying, 'Take and eat: this is my body, given for you. Do this for the remembrance of me.'

"Again, after supper, he took the cup, gave thanks, and gave it for all to drink, saying, 'this cup is the new covenant in my blood, shed for you and for all people for the forgiveness of sin. Do this for remembrance of me'."

THE COMMUNION

THE LORD'S PRAYER

THE PASSING OF THE PEACE

HYMN: *"Fairest Lord Jesus"* or
"Bread of Heaven, on Thee We Feed"

CLOSING PRAYER OF DEDICATION (God So Loved the World, *William Luoma, p. 35)*

O Christ, Lamb of God, it is good for us to be here.
For the gifts you offer at this table, we give you thanks.
We come, and receive, in remembrance of you.
    We come in weakness, and leave with strength;
    We come with anxieties, and experience your peace;
    We come with doubts, and discover the assurance of your love.
For it is in being forgiven that we are able to forgive,
And it is in receiving your love that we are empowered to love others.
Here you provide the nourishment we need for living out our lives of discipleship.
Accept our thanks and praise, for your great love's sake.
Amen

BENEDICTION *(God So Loved the World, William Louma, p. 36)*

May the love of the Lord Jesus draw us to himself;
May the power of the Lord Jesus strengthen us in his service;
May the joy of the Lord Jesus fill our souls, and
May the blessing of God Almighty, the Father, the Son, and
    the Holy Ghost, be upon us and remain with us always.
Amen

POSTLUDE

The Path of Integrity

READER 1

I hate that passage from 1 Corinthians . . .
a little leaven is all you need . . .
asking us to be unleavened bread.
Who wants to be a flat old stale piece
of unleavened bread?
I mean, really, who would want to give up
their leaven . . . the leaven of power . . .
    the leaven of titles . . .
    the leaven of possessions . . .
    the leaven of the good life . . .
    the leaven of popularity or reputation or image?
It is ridiculous to expect anyone to
sincerely consider living a bland — boring — predictable life
as a simple piece of unleavened bread.
What a horrible image . . . what an absurd analogy . . .
what an offensive concept,
to go through life needing only a pinch of leaven.
Maybe if they could make it designer unleavened bread,
then the idea might sell,
it might have a viable market.
Ralph Lauren unleavened bread.
Pierre Cardin unleavened bread.
Bill Blass unleavened bread.
It just might work.

READER 2

What Paul was trying to teach,
was that Christ's own life and ministry
was a symbol of the unleavened life.
Think about it . . . the starkness . . .

the simplicity . . .
the flatness of a life of service . . .
   of sacrifice . . .
   of suffering.
Not much glamour or grandeur in preaching good news to the
poor . . .
   embracing the leper and the beggar . . .
   proclaiming release to the captives . . .
   existing in the midst of squalor . . .
   ministering to the misfit . . .
   living in utter poverty.

Not much comfort and contentment
in the persecuted life of discipleship,
in teaching that the first will be last . . .
   that it will be harder for a rich man to gain entrance into
   heaven, than for a camel to squeeze through the eye of a
   needle . . .
   that the religious elite are really just white washed tombs
   filled with the deadness of deceit and lies.

Not such a luxurious life
to have no titles — no wealth — no stature in the community,
and yet, still ask people to "come unto You for rest . . ."
What an offensive notion that must have been . . .
how totally absurd.

READER 3

In our world today,
there is still no better symbol of the unleavened life
than the act of washing feet.
Dirty, dung encrusted, smelly feet.
Repugnant.
Repulsive.
Revolting.

Yet, the image of Christ washing his disciples' feet
remains a crystalline portrait of integrity,
a picture that clearly portrays Christ's
own lack of care or concern
for the standards and expectations of the world.
Jesus Christ, the footwasher,
stands before us in the glory of his unbloated status . . .
   his deflated image . . .
   his stale flat-looking life,
and reveals the incredible integrity
of standing stripped before the world
as a piece of unleavened bread.

READER 4

We fear the simple starkness of that unleavened life,
even more than we fear the "faith-fact"
that our bloated status as old yeast sinners
now threatens to extinguish the earth's resources . . .
to devour the world in a desperate drive toward a final fire . . .
and to leave us blinded to the myriad "hungers" of our world . . .
for food — for shelter — for protection — for healing — for hope.
We are a people who have lost some of our integrity,
because we have overdosed on yeast.
We are too proud of our bigness . . .
   our grandeur . . .
   our opulence . . .
   our wealth.
Do we know the difference between luxury and necessity?
Do we know how to say no to technology,
if the products of that technology are ecologically or spiritually disastrous?
Can we not understand the hypocrisy of Christianity
when it electronically proclaims that Christ promises the right
to extravagance, a Kingdom not of justice and equality for all,
but a Camelot for a chosen few?

READER 5

Lent is indeed a time when we are compelled . . .
mainly and justifiably . . . by guilt,
to confront the Christ, to open our hearts to Him.
to allow Christ access to our pride and our principles.
Lent is a time when we must stare into that
stark, simple unleavened life, and ask ourselves,
what has happened? . . . Why so much yeast? . . .
Where is our purity? . . . Where is our truth?
It is Lent, and we — if we allow ourselves to be —
are at last in communion with the integrity within ourselves . . .
an integrity first sown by Christ . . . an integrity that is synonymous
with simplicity and obedience and love.
Lent is a revolution, for within this
penitential period we discover the purity and truth of our Selves . . .
our Selves freed of the flab of image and illusion . . .
our Selves stripped of the camouflage of worldly wisdom
and societal standards of success . . .
our Selves finally free to pursue the simple decencies
and acts of compassion and caring and sharing
that give our lives the only satisfaction and integrity
we can ever know or genuinely feel.
As we partake, on this Maundy Thursday,
of a simple stark meal . . . a symbol of obedience and love indeed,
let us be renewed and refreshed by this unleavened supper,
a miracle meal that gives our spirits the needed nourishment'
of becoming disciples whose lives can reflect the integrity of
Jesus Christ. Amen

THE SERVICE FOR GOOD FRIDAY
(A SERVICE OF SILENCES)

SILENT PROCESSIONAL

SILENT MEDITATION *(One minute)*

THE PRAYER OF CONFESSION
Pastor: **WE HAVE BETRAYED YOU!**
People: **We have betrayed you!**
Pastor: Lord, forgive us for our lack of respect for ourselves, and the myriad destructive and even demonic habits we have succumbed to.
People: **WE HAVE BETRAYED YOU!**
Pastor: Lord, forgive us for our mistreatment of friends and family, and our petty jealousies, ridiculous grudges, and simple lack of caring.
People: **WE HAVE BETRAYED YOU!**
Pastor: Lord, forgive us for our lack of compassion for the outcasts of our land, and our neglect of all those broken hearts in need of binding.
People: **WE HAVE BETRAYED YOU!**
Pastor: Lord, forgive us for our tendency to be war preparers and not peacemakers, and to display domination and not dominion over this earth.
People: **WE HAVE BETRAYED YOU!**
Pastor: Lord, forgive us our bigotry that creates chasms, our self-righteous pride which causes hatred, and our God-playing madness which returns us to chaos.
People: **WE HAVE BETRAYED YOU!**
Pastor: Lord, forgive us for our refusal to pray, our defiant denial of Your answers, and our rejection of Your wishes and wants and will for our lives.
People: **WE HAVE BETRAYED YOU!**
Pastor: Lord, forgive us for our calloused hearts that so often crucify the Truth, and our rigid minds which remain closed to Grace.
People: **WE HAVE BETRAYED YOU!**

THE DECLARATION OF PARDON

SILENT MEDITATION *(two minutes)*

HYMN: *"Ah, Holy Jesus, How Have You Offended?"*

OLD TESTAMENT LESSON: *Psalm 130*

SILENT MEDITATION *(three minutes)*

NEW TESTAMENT LESSON: *Hebrews 12:1-14*

SILENT MEDITATION *(four minutes)*

THE GOSPEL: *Luke 23:26-49*

HYMN: *"Were You There, When They Crucified My Lord?"*

SILENT MEDITATION *(five minutes)*

THE SERMON: *"The Path of Dignity"* . . .
  A Dramatic Reading

SILENT MEDITATION *(six minutes)*

CLOSING PRAYER *(in unison)*

   O God, grant us the strength and the sense of deep inner dignity, so that we might pursue the fullness of discipleship. Remind us ceaselessly of the demands . . . the risks . . . the offensiveness . . . the persecution . . . the pain and fear, which comes with picking up our crosses and following you. Let us never forget the serenity and peace, the integrity and maturity, the quality and dignity, which can only be found in a life that is dedicated to Your service. Amen

LORD'S PRAYER

SILENT MEDITATION *(seven minutes)*

HYMN: *"O Sacred Head, Now Wounded"*

THE BENEDICTION

SILENT RECESSIONAL

The Path of Dignity

READER 1

Dignity . . . a word not often used these days.
Dignity . . . a connotation we cannot affix to very many lives.
Dignity . . . a concept that is eroding,
due both to a lack of usage, and a lack
of people worthy of that spiritually significant brand.
Dignity . . . what does the word really mean?
I believe that the term is best explained
by the lesson we heard read from Hebrews, Chapter 12 . . .
"run with determination the race that lies before us" . . .
"eyes fixed on Jesus" . . .
"your struggle against sin" . . .
"do not be discouraged" . . .
"Endure what you suffer" . . .
"disciplined by such punishment" . . .
"strengthen your trembling knees!" . . .
"Keep walking on straight paths" . . .
"be at peace with everyone" . . .
"live a holy life" . . .
these are the attributes that constitute the character of dignity.
Dignity is spiritually bonded,
fused in faith to the qualities of determination . . .
    struggle . . .
    suffering . . .
    strength . . . endurance . . . courage . . .
    righteousness,
and these are the qualities that reflect discipleship.

READER 2

Dignity, as a label, can be applied only
to those lives that strive to be disciples . . .

to live a holy life . . .
to seek first after the Kingdom of God.
Dignity emerges in full regal splendor,
only in those risk taking lives that pick up crosses . . .
    that wear crowns of thorns . . .
    that taste the vinegar.
In a world which revels in the easy life . . .
    which lusts after recreation without re-creation . . .
    which passions for the right to be
    immune to the pains and problems of our lives . . .
dignity is in danger of becoming a word which is obsolete.
The righteous life, the life which pursues
peace and justice and equality and liberty for all . . .
the life which thrives on unconditional loving,
and ceaseless efforts to forgive and to be forgiven . . .
the life which yearns for a closer relationship to God,
and a deeper commitment to the people of the whole world,
such a life is a life of great work . . .
    of great struggle . . .
    of great sacrifice . . .
    of great suffering . . .
    of significant endurance — dedication — determination,
and is not the dream of the person
whose goal is to get away from it all.

READER 3

In all facets of our lives,
we must ask ourselves as to the level of dignity
with which we are functioning, and we must always
    remember that,
"in our struggle against sin
we have not yet had to resist to the point of being killed."
Ultimately, the Cross becomes the acid test of dignity,
the symbol which scorches us with an awareness

of the price tag of the disciplined — determined — dedicated
    life of the disciple . . .
those who choose to run the race.
As individuals we must face the Cross inspired scrutiny
of our laziness, and the sin of our quest for the good life,
a good life that ironically keeps us out of the race almost
    totally.
In friendship and within the family,
we must address the issues of pride — selfishness —
the refusal to forgive, or be forgiven — the Demolition Derbies
of jealousy and anger and hurt — our lack of awareness and
    attention
to the wishes and needs and dreams
of those we claim to love,
and we must do so from the penetrating and piercing
perspective of the Cross.
Across the board, the Cross is the acid test of dignity,
and the clear and ever-present reminder
that dignity is earned only by those
individuals . . . families . . . friendships . . . marriages . . .
    even nations,
that are willing to run the race with their eyes glued
on Jesus Christ . . . the crucified Messiah . . . the persecuted
    Prince of Peace.

On this Good Friday,
let us keep in focus
the centrality of the Cross to our faiths . . .
    to our lives . . .
        to the level of dignity we attain.
Amen

THE SERVICE FOR EASTER DAY

PRELUDE

CALL TO WORSHIP
Pastor: We come together this Easter morning with a spirit of joy and a deep feeling of thanksgiving.
People: **We come here with humble hearts, ready both to confess fully and celebrate sincerely.**
All: *It is Easter morning, and we are here ready and willing to genuinely worship. Amen*

HYMN: *"I Danced in the Morning (Lord of the Dance)"*

PRAYER OF CONFESSION
Pastor: We are conscious, Lord, that you have called us often to place our faith in you, to feel total trust in your prayer, to guide and direct our lives.
People: **Forgive us, Lord, for our failure to have an Easter faith, a faith which embraces ourselves, others and our God with an enthusiasm and excitement for just being alive.**
Pastor: We are conscious, Lord, that you have called us often to have abundant hope, to plunge into the future brimming with the wish for peace and harmony in our world.
People: **Forgive us, Lord, for our failure to have that Easter hope, a hope that can indeed move mountains, a hope that is built upon wisdom and truth.**
Pastor: We are conscious, Lord, that you have called us often to make loving our top priority, to know that to love is our greatest gift to give, our mission in life.
People: **Forgive us, Lord, for our failure to have that Easter love, a love which is reckless and risk-taking in the name of Christ.**

THE DECLARATION OF PARDON

RESPONSIVE READING: *Psalm 91*
He who dwells in the shelter of the Most High, who abides in the shadow of the Almighty, will say to the Lord, "My

refuge and my fortress; my God, in whom I trust."
For he will deliver you from the snare of the fowler and from the deadly pestilence;
He will cover you with his pinions, and under his wings you will find refuge;
His faithfulness is a shield and buckler
You will not fear the terror of the night,
Nor the arrow that flies by day,
Nor the pestilence that talks in darkness,
Nor the destruction that wastes at noonday.
A thousand may fall at your side, ten thousand at your right hand; but it will not come near you.
You will only look with your eyes and see the recompense of the wicked.
Because you have made the Lord your refuge, the Most High your habitation,
No evil shall befall you, no scourge come near your tent.
For he will give his angels charge of you to guard you in all your ways.
On their hands they will bear you up, lest you dash your foot against a stone.
You will tread on the lion and the adder,
The young lion and the serpent you will trample under foot.
Because he cleaves to me in love, I will deliver him;
I will protect him, because he knows my name.
When he calls to me, I will answer him; I will be with him in trouble, I will rescue him and honor him.
With long life I will satisfy him, and show him my salvation.

ANTHEM / SOLO

UNISON READING: *Romans 12:1, 2, 9-21*

I appeal to you therefore, brethren, by the mercies of God, to present your bodies as a living sacrifice, holy and acceptable to God, which is your spiritual worship. Do not be conformed to this world but be transformed by the renewal of your mind, that you may prove what is the will of God, what is good and acceptable and perfect.

Let love be genuine; hate what is evil, hold fast to what is good; love one another with brotherly affection; outdo one another in showing honor. Never flag in zeal, be aglow with the Spirit, serve the Lord. Rejoice in your hope, be patient in tribulation, be constant in prayer. Contribute to the needs of the saints, practice hospitality.

Bless those who persecute you; bless and do not curse them. Rejoice with those who rejoice, weep with those who weep. Live in harmony with one another; do not be haughty, but associate with the lowly; never be conceited. Repay no one evil for evil, but take thought for what is noble in the sight of all. If possible, so far as it depends upon you, live peaceably with all. Beloved, never avenge yourselves, but leave it to the wrath of God; for it is written, "Vengence is mine. I will repay, says the Lord." No, "if your enemy is hungry, feed him; if he is thirsty, give him drink; for by so doing you will heap burning coals upon his head." Do not be overcome by evil, but overcome evil with good.

THE SCRIPTURE LESSON: *Luke 24:1-12*

SERMON: *"The Path of Creativity"* . . . *A Dramatic Reading*

HYMN: *"Beautiful Savior"* or
"Christ the Lord is Risen Today"

THE EASTER CREED

We believe in a present and powerful Christ,
a Christ who daily fills our lives with the Truth,
the Truth that frees us to see beauty,
the Truth that frees us to love without conditions,
the Truth that frees us to live out our convictions.

We believe in a forgiving and forgetting Christ,
a Christ who daily reminds that we have
the right and the responsibility to a fresh start,
the right and responsibility to live out our Baptism,
the right and the responsibility to commune with the Lord of Grace.

We believe in a mysterious and magnificent Christ,
a Christ who daily awes us with the splendor of creation, and
the unparalleled beauty of living and learning,
the unparalleled beauty of giving and caring,
the unparalleled beauty of knowing that Easter is REAL.

LITANY FOR WORLD PEACE *(From* The Worshipbook, *Westminster Press, 1970 Joint Committee on Worship for Presbyterian Churches, pp. 125-126.)*

Leader: O God our Father: we pray for all your children on earth, of every nation and of every race; that they may be strong to do your will.

We pray for the church in the world.

People: **Give peace in our time, O Lord.**
Leader: For the United Nations;
People: **Give peace in our time, O Lord.**
Leader: For international federations of labor, industry and commerce;
People: **Give peace in our time, O Lord.**
Leader: For departments of state, ambassadors, diplomats, and statesmen;
People: **Give peace in our time, O Lord.**
Leader: For worldwide agencies of compassion, which bind wounds and feed the hungry;
People: **Give peace in our time, O Lord.**
Leader: For all who in any way work to further the cause of peace and goodwill;
People: **Give peace in our time, O Lord.**
Leader: For common folk in every land who live in peace;
People: **Give peace in our time, O Lord.**
Leader: Eternal God: use us, even our ignorance and weakness, to bring about your holy will. Hurry the day when people shall live together in your love; for yours is the kingdom, the power, and the glory forever.
People: **Amen**

ORDER FOR AN AGAPE

(This "love feast" should be a special breakfast, and the congregation should be encouraged to bring homemade breads and rolls and pastries.)

(From The Worshipbook, *Westminster Press, 1970 Joint Committee on Worship for Presbyterian Churches, pp. 62-64.)*

The Agape, or "love feast," is a fellowship meal that should not be confused with the Lord's Supper. The Agape recalls meals Jesus shared with disciples during his ministry, and is an expression of the fellowship that

Christians enjoy when they meet as "the household of God."

The Agape may be held at table, and be conducted by members of the congregation, or by the minister assisted by members of the congregation. Families may bring dishes of food to the table for all to share.

Let the leader say:

Praise to you, O Lord our God, king of the universe, who causes the earth to yield food for all,

Or

Give thanks to the Lord, for he is good,
His love is everlasting!
Give thanks to the God of gods
His love is everlasting!
Give thanks to the Lord of lords,
His love is everlasting!

Hymn "Jesus Christ Is Risen Today" — may be sung, after which the leader may greet the people, welcoming them as friends in Christ.

Then, let a reader read Luke 9:12-17. The leader shall pray, saying:

Let us pray.

Great God, our Father, whose Son Jesus broke bread to feed a crowd in Galilee: we thank you for the food you give us. May we enjoy your gifts thankfully, and share what we have with brothers on earth who hunger and thirst, giving praise to Jesus Christ, who has shown your perfect love. Amen

Appropriately, there may be five loaves of bread. The leader may break one of them, and, after taking a piece of bread, may pass the broken halves, one to the left and the other to the right. The remaining loaves may be distributed to all the people.

Then, the people shall eat bread, and pass their dishes of food. People may talk together as neighbors in faith; or the leader may direct their conversations by suggesting matters of mutual concern.

When the meal is ended, a reader may read one or more or the following passages, or some other appropriate lesson from Scripture:
    Matthew 22:34-40

Luke 14:16-24
1 Corinthians 13
2 Corinthians 9:6-15
Philippians 2:5-11

Then let the leader say:

Let us pray.

We praise you, God our creator, for your good gifts to us and all mankind. We thank you for the friendship we have in Christ: and for the promise of your coming kingdom, where there will be no more hunger and thirst, and where men will be satisfied by your love. As this bread was once seed scattered on earth to be gathered into one loaf, so may your church be joined together into one holy people, who praise you for your love made known in Jesus Christ the Lord. Amen

My dear people, we are already children of God. His commandments are these: that we believe in his Son Jesus Christ, and that we love one another. Whoever keeps his commandments lives in God and God lives in him. We know he lives in us by the Spirit he has given us.

Or,

My dear people, since God loved us so much, we too should love one another. No one has ever seen God; but as long as we love one another God will live in us, and his love will be complete in us.

The people may sing the Doxology.

Then the leader shall say:

Let us show our love for neighbors.

The leader may wish to announce a particular need to which the people may give. Baskets may be passed around the table so that the people may contribute. A hymn may be sung as the collection is taken, or after the collection has been taken.

The Lord's Prayer shall be said:

Our Father . . .
The Agape may conclude with a dismissal:

Go in peace. The grace of the Lord Jesus Christ be with you all. Amen

The Path of Creativity

READER 1

The Resurrection is not . . .
I repeat . . . NOT . . .
something which happens only at the time of death,
nor is it an event that only has impact on our dying.
If the Resurrection was important
only in terms of what happens beyond Life,
and had no real impact or power over
what happens during our lives, well,
I guess I can honestly say that, then,
I would have little use for a faith built
on such a "post-living" concept or event.
Resurrection that cannot transform the present . . .
Resurrection that cannot heal our NOW . .
Resurrection that cannot create new hope and new being
　　TODAY,
is a Resurrection that falls flat on its hollow, excessively
　　righteous face.
Easter is a day when we celebrate, not as a
means of preparing for THE END . . .
not as a means of affirming that there is something
　　BEYOND . . .
not as a means of acknowledging that there is an escape hatch
　　to Death's door,
but we celebrate because the Resurrection
can so radically and totally rearrange . . .
　　　renew . . .
　　　restore . . .
　　　revamp . . .
　　　rekindle, our spirits —
　　　　　our dreams —
　　　　　our hopes —
　　　　　our lives.

READER 2

The Resurrection isn't some religious theory
to free us from the anxiety of dying,
or to offer us a guaranteed immortality.
The Resurrection offers us the freedom of
becoming brand new in Jesus Christ,
the freedom of actualizing our baptism,
the freedom of faith . . . a faith which knows that
    the power of Christ —
    the love of Christ —
    the forgiveness of Christ —
    the healing of Christ —
    the hope of Christ,
is all available to us everywhere . . . all of the time . . . to
    everyone.
The conquering of Death,
the robbing Death of its sting,
is not something which we win by our own death . . .
is not a victory sealed with our own coffins,
but is won whenever we choose to have Life,
and to have it abundantly.

READER 3

We defeat Death,
whenever we defiantly celebrate the dignity and integrity of
Life.

We conquer Death,
whenever we embrace our own Grace-created capacity
to be forever new.

We vanquish Death,
whenever we choose to live as the serving and sacrificing
disciples we were created to be.
We watch Death shrivel up and collapse in futility,
whenever we have the courage and the conviction

to become peacemakers . . .
to forgive and be forgiven . . .
to make a commitment and keep it . . .
to speak out for an end to oppression and greed . . .
to demand that the hungry be fed —
    the homeless be found homes —
    the imprisoned be given hope . . .
to live lives that reflect mercy and justice —
    that grant others both respect and compassion —
    that believe in the healing powers of love . . .
to dream dreams that will build the Kingdom,
and not dreams that construct an artificial Camelot . . .
to have a vision of a safer —
    a saner —
    a simpler world . . .
to reject bigotry . . .
to abhor idolatries . . .
to claim our failures and our flaws . . .
to embrace the evil of this world
with a faith that believes that the Good will indeed emerge
    victorious . . .
to know that Death is ultimately defeated
by lives that are lived with great strength . . .
    focused priorities . . .
    solid principles . . .
    disciplined efforts . . .
    and a Grace-dependent faith.

READER 4

If Resurrection only promised a life after death,
and not a new life before death,
it would be *the idle tale* that even the disciples could not believe.
It is when the Resurrection becomes the source —
    the well —
    the catalyst of creativity . . .
        of creative living,
that the Resurrection becomes an event bursting and

    blossoming forth with eternal possibilities and
       potentialities.

The Resurrection, the eternal creator of new life,
the eternal force that empowers our own creativity . . .
    our own capacity to resolve conflicts . . .
    our own capacity to dream —
       to wish —
       to hope . . .
    our own capacity to transform
    friendships — families — feelings . . .
    our own capacity to believe
    even when the world proclaims our belief
    as that of a someone
    who is the perpetual fool.
The Resurrection . . . the creative spirit . . .
    the generator of new life . . .
    the igniter of new hope . . .
    the author of all genuine creativity,
is an eternal event with dramatic consequences
for the moment . . . for the NOW . . . for TODAY.
It is the Resurrection which creates the faithful spirit,
a spirit which seizes the present with the revolutionary belief
that anything is possible . . .
that peace can be made . . .
that equality can be lived . . .
that justice can reign . . .
that the rainbow can be seen in the rain . . .
that everything is new under the Son of God.
Resurrection, the eternal flame of creativity,
    the creative force of NEW LIFE,
    the creative faith of a Death defeating
    energy and exuberance for being
    fully and eternally alive . . .
    fully and eternally human . . .
    fully and eternally God's. AMEN

www.ingramcontent.com/pod-product-compliance
Lightning Source LLC
Chambersburg PA
CBHW071758040426
42446CB00012B/2609